U.S. PRESIDENTS

D0002238

The United States Presidents

JOHN TYLER

ABDO Publishing Company

Megan M. Gunderson

visit us at
www.abdopublishing.com

Cover Photo: Getty Images
Interior Photos: Alamy p. 10; Corbis pp. 11, 25, 29; Getty Images pp. 13, 15, 19, 21; iStockphoto pp. 16, 32; Library of Congress pp. 5, 9, 17, 18, 23, 24; National Archives p. 26; Picture History p. 27

Editor: BreAnn Rumsch
Art Direction & Cover Design: Neil Klinepier
Interior Design: Neil Klinepier

Library of Congress Cataloging-in-Publication Data

Gunderson, Megan M., 1981-
  John Tyler / Megan M. Gunderson.
       p. cm. -- (The United States presidents)
  Includes index.
  ISBN 978-1-60453-477-1
  1. Tyler, John, 1790-1862--Juvenile literature. 2. Presidents--United States--Biography--Juvenile literature. I. Title.

  E397.G86 2009
  973.5'8092--dc22
  [B]
                                    2008027053

CONTENTS

JOHN TYLER

John Tyler was born in Virginia in 1790. At the age of 19, he became a lawyer. Later, he served in both houses of Congress. Tyler also was governor of Virginia.

In 1840, Tyler was elected vice president under William H. Harrison. Just one month after taking office, President Harrison died. At the time, there had been just nine U.S. presidents. None had ever died in office before.

The U.S. **Constitution** was unclear about what should happen next. Some people thought the vice president should just act as president. Others thought he should officially become the next president. Tyler agreed and took the presidential oath of office. This set the standard for future vice presidents facing similar situations.

Tyler's situation caused trouble with Congress and his **cabinet**. Yet he still accomplished much as president. Tyler helped settle a border disagreement with Great Britain. He also admitted Florida as a state. After one term, President Tyler retired. He became active in politics again before his death in 1862.

TIMELINE

1790 - On March 29, John Tyler was born in Charles City County, Virginia.

1807 - Tyler graduated from the College of William and Mary.

1809 - Tyler became a lawyer.

1811 - At age 21, Tyler was elected to the Virginia House of Delegates.

1813 - Tyler led a company of Charles City County militia during the War of 1812; he married Letitia Christian on March 29.

1816 - Tyler was elected to the U.S. House of Representatives.

1823 - Tyler returned to the Virginia House of Delegates.

1825 - Tyler became governor of Virginia.

1827 - Tyler was elected to the U.S. Senate.

1836 - Tyler quit the U.S. Senate; he ran for vice president, but lost.

1840 - Tyler was elected vice president under William H. Harrison.

1841 - On April 4, President Harrison died; Tyler became the tenth U.S. president on April 6.

1842 - Letitia Tyler died on September 10.

1844 - Tyler married Julia Gardiner.

1861 - The American Civil War began; Tyler was elected to the Confederate House of Representatives.

1862 - On January 18, John Tyler died.

DID YOU KNOW?

John Tyler had 15 children. That is more than any president before or since!

Julia Tyler gets credit for a famous presidential tradition. She began having the president greeted with the song "Hail to the Chief." Today, it is played when the president arrives at formal occasions.

When Tyler became president, he was 51 years old. At the time, he was the youngest ever to hold that office.

Letitia Tyler was the first president's wife to die in the White House. Later, Tyler became the first president to marry while in office.

VIRGINIA CHILDHOOD

John Tyler was born on March 29, 1790, in Charles City County, Virginia. He was born on a plantation called Greenway. Greenway is on the James River. It is just south of the state capital, Richmond.

John's father was also named John. He had attended the College of William and Mary in Williamsburg, Virginia. There, he had been a roommate of the third U.S. president, Thomas Jefferson. John became a judge and later served as governor of Virginia. He and Mary Armistead had eight children. Young John was their sixth child and second son.

From a young age, John was successful. In school, he fought back against a violent teacher. Still, he was a good student. John had blue eyes and light brown hair. He was slim and grew to be six feet (2 m) tall.

FAST FACTS

BORN - March 29, 1790
WIVES - Letitia Christian (1790–1842), Julia Gardiner (1820–1889)
CHILDREN - 15
POLITICAL PARTY - Whig
AGE AT INAUGURATION - 51
YEARS SERVED - 1841–1845
VICE PRESIDENT - None
DIED - January 18, 1862, age 71

John's birthplace in Charles City County

SCHOOL DAYS

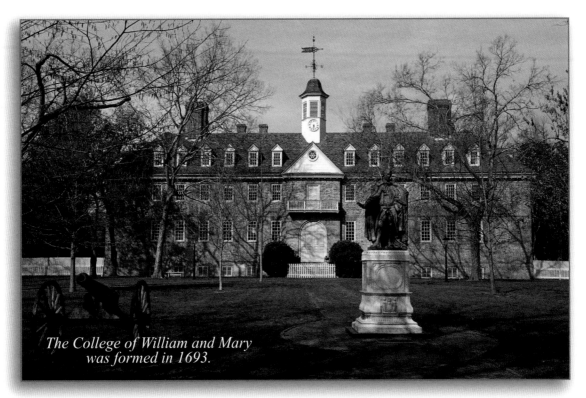

*The College of William and Mary
was formed in 1693.*

In 1802, John entered the College of William and Mary. He studied ancient history, Latin, Greek, poetry, and political subjects. John liked to write poetry and play violin in his free time.

John graduated from college in 1807. He then studied law with his father. In 1808, John's father became governor of Virginia. John decided to move to Richmond with the new governor.

There, John studied law under Edmund Randolph. Randolph had been the first U.S. **attorney general** under President George Washington. John also joined a **debating** society to practice arguing cases. In 1809, he became a lawyer.

George Washington (far left) *with his first cabinet. The members are* (left to right) *Secretary of War Henry Knox, Secretary of the Treasury Alexander Hamilton, Secretary of State Thomas Jefferson, and Attorney General Edmund Randolph.*

FAMILY MAN

Tyler quickly became a successful lawyer. Yet he was also interested in politics. In 1811, Tyler was elected to the Virginia House of Delegates. He was just 21 years old.

The next year, the **War of 1812** started. Tyler supported this struggle against Great Britain. In 1813, he led a company of Charles City County **militia**. They organized to defend Richmond and areas nearby in case of British attacks.

That same year, Tyler married Letitia Christian. They had met in 1808. Tyler had grown up just a few miles from Letitia's family plantation. The wedding took place on Tyler's twenty-third birthday. The couple lived at Greenway. They eventually had eight children.

When Letitia Tyler (right) later moved into the White House, she was too ill to serve as hostess. Her daughter-in-law Priscilla Cooper Tyler performed her public duties instead.

CONGRESSMAN TYLER

In 1816, Tyler was elected to the U.S. House of Representatives. Tyler believed the government's powers were limited to those listed in the U.S. **Constitution**. So, he fought against several important issues in Congress.

The Bank of the United States had first been created in 1791. It was to last for 20 years. Then in 1816, it formed again. The bank gave loans to the national government and state banks. Tyler did not believe Congress had the power to form this bank. He felt this went against the Constitution. So, he spoke out against it.

Congressman Tyler also voted against the Missouri Compromise of 1820. The compromise decided how far slavery could spread in the United States. Tyler himself was a slave owner. He felt the national government and the Northern states should not interfere with slavery. Still, the compromise passed.

For four years, Tyler worked in Congress. He left in 1821 because of poor health. After getting his strength back, Tyler returned to the Virginia House of Delegates. He served there from 1823 to 1825.

Tyler's excellent speaking skills helped him in his political career.

DEMOCRATIC SENATOR

The Executive Mansion has been home to Virginia governors, including Tyler, since 1813.

In 1825, the Virginia state legislature chose Tyler to be governor. As governor, he supported improving railroads and canals. The following year, former president Thomas Jefferson died on July 4. As governor, Tyler gave the official state **eulogy**. This speech praised Jefferson, who had been a role model for Tyler.

Tyler was elected to the U.S. Senate in 1827. He supported **Democrat** Andrew Jackson for president in 1828 and 1832. President Jackson was against the Bank of the United States. So, he removed some government money from it.

As a fellow Democrat, Tyler still did not support the Bank of the United States. However, Tyler could not support Jackson's actions either. Many felt the president did not have the **constitutional** power to remove the money. So in 1834, Tyler voted to **censure** Jackson.

President Andrew Jackson served two terms, from 1829 to 1837.

In 1836, the Virginia legislature told Tyler to change his vote. Tyler refused. Instead, he quit the Senate that year. He then returned home to practice law.

WHIG CANDIDATE

In 1834, a new political party had formed. It was called the **Whig** Party. The Whigs disapproved of President Jackson and his policies.

The Whig Party liked Tyler because he had been against Jackson. In 1836, the Whigs had several candidates for president and vice president. Tyler ran for vice president, but lost.

In 1839, the Whig Party chose William H. Harrison to run for president. People liked Harrison because of his military experience. He had won the Battle of Tippecanoe against the Shawnee Native Americans in 1811. And, he had fought in the **War of 1812**.

Harrison was also born in Charles City County.

Harrison had become a hero of the western frontier. Yet the **Whigs** also needed Southern votes to win the election. Tyler had support in the South. So, the Whigs asked him to run for vice president.

Tyler returned to his successful law practice between the 1836 and 1840 elections.

TIPPECANOE AND TYLER, TOO

The 1840 campaign changed the way political campaigns were run. During the campaign, the candidates avoided discussing political issues. Instead, the **Whigs** and the **Democrats** used **slogans** and songs to get votes.

Harrison's nickname was "Old Tippecanoe" in honor of his famous battle victory. So, the Whig campaign slogan was "Tippecanoe and Tyler, Too." The slogan was fun to say. And, it made the candidates easy to remember.

Voters did not know what ideas Harrison and Tyler stood for. Still, the Whigs won the election. They defeated Democratic president Martin Van Buren.

On March 4, 1841, Harrison took office. Sadly, he became ill soon after his **inauguration**. William H. Harrison died on April 4, 1841. He had been in office for just one month.

When Tyler took office, he was already an experienced politician.

Becoming President

A president had never died in office before. So, nobody was certain what should happen next. However, the U.S. **Constitution** does say what to do if a president cannot perform the duties of his or her office. It states that "the Same shall **devolve** on the Vice President."

Still, people disagreed about exactly what these words meant. Tyler's **cabinet** and other leaders thought the vice president should simply act as president. Others said the vice president should actually become president.

Tyler believed it was his constitutional right to become president. So, he claimed the office of president and all of its powers and responsibilities.

On April 6, 1841, Tyler took the presidential oath of office. Then, Congress officially recognized his right to remain in office as president. The cabinet agreed. Tyler's successful fight set the course for future vice presidents. They too would assume the power of the presidency if a president died.

Tyler's opponents nicknamed him "His Accidency."

PRESIDENT TYLER

Tyler often disagreed with Congress while he was president. Congress passed two bills relating to forming a new Bank of the United States. Tyler believed the bills were **unconstitutional**. So, he stopped both of them.

Afterward, Tyler's entire **cabinet** except **Secretary of State** Daniel Webster resigned. They hoped to force Tyler out of office. But Tyler was prepared. He chose new cabinet members within two days! However, **Whig** leaders were still upset with Tyler. So in 1841, they removed him from the party.

Soon, Tyler faced personal tragedy. On September 10, 1842, Letitia Tyler died. She had been ill for some time. Happily, Tyler soon fell in love with Julia Gardiner. They married two years later and had seven children together.

Daniel Webster was secretary of state under three presidents. They were William H. Harrison, John Tyler, and Millard Fillmore.

PRESIDENT TYLER'S CABINET

**APRIL 6, 1841–
MARCH 4, 1845**

- **STATE –** Daniel Webster
  Abel P. Upshur (from July 24, 1843)
  John C. Calhoun (from April 1, 1844)
- **TREASURY –** Thomas Ewing
  Walter Forward (from September 13, 1841)
  John C. Spencer (from March 8, 1843)
  George M. Bibb (from July 4, 1844)
- **WAR –** John Bell
  John C. Spencer (from October 12, 1841)
  James M. Porter (from March 8, 1843)
  William Wilkins (from February 20, 1844)
- **NAVY –** George Edmund Badger
  Abel P. Upshur (from October 11, 1841)
  David Henshaw (from July 24, 1843)
  Thomas W. Gilmer (from February 19, 1844)
  John Y. Mason (from March 26, 1844)
- **ATTORNEY GENERAL –** John Jordan Crittenden
  Hugh S. Legaré (from September 20, 1841)
  John Nelson (from July 1, 1843)

Tyler approved the
Webster-Ashburton Treaty
in August 1842.

Despite his battles with Congress, President Tyler had many successes in office. In 1842, the government ended the Second Seminole War in Florida. Three years later, Tyler signed a bill admitting Florida as a state. He also worked toward **annexing** Texas.

As President, Tyler helped settle a boundary issue with Great Britain. In 1842, this led to the Webster-Ashburton Treaty. It is named for **Secretary of State** Daniel Webster. He worked on the treaty with Britain's Alexander Baring, 1st Baron Ashburton. The treaty established the international border between Maine and Canada.

Tyler also wished to improve trade relations with other countries. So in 1844, the United States signed a treaty with China. The Treaty of Wangxia opened trade between the two nations.

Julia Tyler also worked for the annexation of Texas.

AFTER THE WHITE HOUSE

Despite his successes, no political party nominated Tyler for a second term. In 1844, he supported **Democratic** candidate James K. Polk. Polk won the election. The following March, Tyler left office.

When Tyler left the White House, his family moved to Sherwood Forest. Like Greenway, this plantation is in Charles City County. Tyler lived there quietly for many years.

Meanwhile, Americans were arguing more and more about slavery. So in 1861, Tyler led a conference. There, people tried to find a solution for the arguing states. However, the Senate rejected their proposals. Tyler feared the South would split from the North. He argued against such a decision. But he did not succeed.

Just before Abraham Lincoln became president in 1861, seven Southern states **seceded**. They formed a new country called the Confederate States of America. Soon, the American **Civil War** began.

Tyler was elected to the Confederate House of Representatives. Yet before he could take his position, he died. On January 18, 1862, John Tyler passed away in Richmond.

Tyler achieved much during his presidency despite opposition. He will always be remembered as the first vice president to become president because of another's death. John Tyler's successful fight to become president set the standard for future vice presidents.

Like Greenway, Sherwood Forest is on the James River.

OFFICE OF THE PRESIDENT

BRANCHES OF GOVERNMENT

The U.S. government is divided into three branches. They are the executive, legislative, and judicial branches. This division is called a separation of powers. Each branch has some power over the others. This is called a system of checks and balances.

EXECUTIVE BRANCH

The executive branch enforces laws. It is made up of the president, the vice president, and the president's cabinet. The president represents the United States around the world. He or she oversees relations with other countries and signs treaties. The president signs bills into law and appoints officials and federal judges. He or she also leads the military and manages government workers.

LEGISLATIVE BRANCH

The legislative branch makes laws, maintains the military, and regulates trade. It also has the power to declare war. This branch consists of the Senate and the House of Representatives. Together, these two houses make up Congress. Each state has two senators. A state's population determines the number of representatives it has.

JUDICIAL BRANCH

The judicial branch interprets laws. It consists of district courts, courts of appeals, and the Supreme Court. District courts try cases. If a person disagrees with a trial's outcome, he or she may appeal. If the courts of appeals support the ruling, a person may appeal to the Supreme Court. The Supreme Court also makes sure that laws follow the U.S. Constitution.

QUALIFICATIONS FOR OFFICE

To be president, a person must meet three requirements. A candidate must be at least 35 years old and a natural-born U.S. citizen. He or she must also have lived in the United States for at least 14 years.

ELECTORAL COLLEGE

The U.S. presidential election is an indirect election. Voters from each state choose electors to represent them in the Electoral College. The number of electors from each state is based on population. Each elector has one electoral vote. Electors are pledged to cast their vote for the candidate who receives the highest number of popular votes in their state. A candidate must receive the majority of Electoral College votes to win.

TERM OF OFFICE

Each president may be elected to two four-year terms. Sometimes, a president may only be elected once. This happens if he or she served more than two years of the previous president's term.

The presidential election is held on the Tuesday after the first Monday in November. The president is sworn in on January 20 of the following year. At that time, he or she takes the oath of office:

I do solemnly swear (or affirm) that I will faithfully execute the office of President of the United States, and will to the best of my ability, preserve, protect and defend the Constitution of the United States.

Line of Succession

The Presidential Succession Act of 1947 defines who becomes president if the president cannot serve. The vice president is first in the line of succession. Next are the Speaker of the House and the President Pro Tempore of the Senate. If none of these individuals is able to serve, the office falls to the president's cabinet members. They would take office in the order in which each department was created:

| Secretary of State |
| Secretary of the Treasury |
| Secretary of Defense |
| Attorney General |
| Secretary of the Interior |
| Secretary of Agriculture |
| Secretary of Commerce |
| Secretary of Labor |
| Secretary of Health and Human Services |
| Secretary of Housing and Urban Development |
| Secretary of Transportation |
| Secretary of Energy |
| Secretary of Education |
| Secretary of Veterans Affairs |
| Secretary of Homeland Security |

BENEFITS

• While in office, the president receives a salary of $400,000 each year. He or she lives in the White House and has 24-hour Secret Service protection.

• The president may travel on a Boeing 747 jet called Air Force One. The airplane can accommodate 70 passengers. It has kitchens, a dining room, sleeping areas, and a conference room. It also has fully equipped offices with the latest communications systems. Air Force One can fly halfway around the world before needing to refuel. It can even refuel in flight!

• If the president wishes to travel by car, he or she uses Cadillac One. Cadillac One is a Cadillac Deville. It has been modified with heavy armor and communications systems. The president takes Cadillac One along when visiting other countries if secure transportation will be needed.

• The president also travels on a helicopter called Marine One. Like the presidential car, Marine One accompanies the president when traveling abroad if necessary.

• Sometimes, the president needs to get away and relax with family and friends. Camp David is the official presidential retreat. It is located in the cool, wooded mountains in Maryland. The U.S. Navy maintains the retreat, and the U.S. Marine Corps keeps it secure. The camp offers swimming, tennis, golf, and hiking.

• When the president leaves office, he or she receives Secret Service protection for ten more years. He or she also receives a yearly pension of $191,300 and funding for office space, supplies, and staff.

PRESIDENTS AND THEIR TERMS

PRESIDENT	PARTY	TOOK OFFICE	LEFT OFFICE	TERMS SERVED	VICE PRESIDENT
George Washington	None	April 30, 1789	March 4, 1797	Two	John Adams
John Adams	Federalist	March 4, 1797	March 4, 1801	One	Thomas Jefferson
Thomas Jefferson	Democratic-Republican	March 4, 1801	March 4, 1809	Two	Aaron Burr, George Clinton
James Madison	Democratic-Republican	March 4, 1809	March 4, 1817	Two	George Clinton, Elbridge Gerry
James Monroe	Democratic-Republican	March 4, 1817	March 4, 1825	Two	Daniel D. Tompkins
John Quincy Adams	Democratic-Republican	March 4, 1825	March 4, 1829	One	John C. Calhoun
Andrew Jackson	Democrat	March 4, 1829	March 4, 1837	Two	John C. Calhoun, Martin Van Buren
Martin Van Buren	Democrat	March 4, 1837	March 4, 1841	One	Richard M. Johnson
William H. Harrison	Whig	March 4, 1841	April 4, 1841	Died During First Term	John Tyler
John Tyler	Whig	April 6, 1841	March 4, 1845	Completed Harrison's Term	Office Vacant
James K. Polk	Democrat	March 4, 1845	March 4, 1849	One	George M. Dallas
Zachary Taylor	Whig	March 5, 1849	July 9, 1850	Died During First Term	Millard Fillmore

PRESIDENT	PARTY	TOOK OFFICE	LEFT OFFICE	TERMS SERVED	VICE PRESIDENT
Millard Fillmore	Whig	July 10, 1850	March 4, 1853	Completed Taylor's Term	Office Vacant
Franklin Pierce	Democrat	March 4, 1853	March 4, 1857	One	William R.D. King
James Buchanan	Democrat	March 4, 1857	March 4, 1861	One	John C. Breckinridge
Abraham Lincoln	Republican	March 4, 1861	April 15, 1865	Served One Term, Died During Second Term	Hannibal Hamlin, Andrew Johnson
Andrew Johnson	Democrat	April 15, 1865	March 4, 1869	Completed Lincoln's Second Term	Office Vacant
Ulysses S. Grant	Republican	March 4, 1869	March 4, 1877	Two	Schuyler Colfax, Henry Wilson
Rutherford B. Hayes	Republican	March 3, 1877	March 4, 1881	One	William A. Wheeler
James A. Garfield	Republican	March 4, 1881	September 19, 1881	Died During First Term	Chester Arthur
Chester Arthur	Republican	September 20, 1881	March 4, 1885	Completed Garfield's Term	Office Vacant
Grover Cleveland	Democrat	March 4, 1885	March 4, 1889	One	Thomas A. Hendricks
Benjamin Harrison	Republican	March 4, 1889	March 4, 1893	One	Levi P. Morton
Grover Cleveland	Democrat	March 4, 1893	March 4, 1897	One	Adlai E. Stevenson
William McKinley	Republican	March 4, 1897	September 14, 1901	Served One Term, Died During Second Term	Garret A. Hobart, Theodore Roosevelt

PRESIDENT	PARTY	TOOK OFFICE	LEFT OFFICE	TERMS SERVED	VICE PRESIDENT
Theodore Roosevelt	Republican	September 14, 1901	March 4, 1909	Completed McKinley's Second Term, Served One Term	Office Vacant, Charles Fairbanks
William Taft	Republican	March 4, 1909	March 4, 1913	One	James S. Sherman
Woodrow Wilson	Democrat	March 4, 1913	March 4, 1921	Two	Thomas R. Marshall
Warren G. Harding	Republican	March 4, 1921	August 2, 1923	Died During First Term	Calvin Coolidge
Calvin Coolidge	Republican	August 3, 1923	March 4, 1929	Completed Harding's Term, Served One Term	Office Vacant, Charles Dawes
Herbert Hoover	Republican	March 4, 1929	March 4, 1933	One	Charles Curtis
Franklin D. Roosevelt	Democrat	March 4, 1933	April 12, 1945	Served Three Terms, Died During Fourth Term	John Nance Garner, Henry A. Wallace, Harry S. Truman
Harry S. Truman	Democrat	April 12, 1945	January 20, 1953	Completed Roosevelt's Fourth Term, Served One Term	Office Vacant, Alben Barkley
Dwight D. Eisenhower	Republican	January 20, 1953	January 20, 1961	Two	Richard Nixon
John F. Kennedy	Democrat	January 20, 1961	November 22, 1963	Died During First Term	Lyndon B. Johnson
Lyndon B. Johnson	Democrat	November 22, 1963	January 20, 1969	Completed Kennedy's Term, Served One Term	Office Vacant, Hubert H. Humphrey
Richard Nixon	Republican	January 20, 1969	August 9, 1974	Completed First Term, Resigned During Second Term	Spiro T. Agnew, Gerald Ford

PRESIDENT	PARTY	TOOK OFFICE	LEFT OFFICE	TERMS SERVED	VICE PRESIDENT
Gerald Ford	Republican	August 9, 1974	January 20, 1977	Completed Nixon's Second Term	Nelson A. Rockefeller
Jimmy Carter	Democrat	January 20, 1977	January 20, 1981	One	Walter Mondale
Ronald Reagan	Republican	January 20, 1981	January 20, 1989	Two	George H.W. Bush
George H.W. Bush	Republican	January 20, 1989	January 20, 1993	One	Dan Quayle
Bill Clinton	Democrat	January 20, 1993	January 20, 2001	Two	Al Gore
George W. Bush	Republican	January 20, 2001	January 20, 2009	Two	Dick Cheney
Barack Obama	Democrat	January 20, 2009			Joe Biden

"We are in the enjoyment of all the blessings of civil and religious liberty." John Tyler

WRITE TO THE PRESIDENT

You may write to the president at:

The White House
1600 Pennsylvania Avenue NW
Washington, DC 20500

You may e-mail the president at:
comments@whitehouse.gov

GLOSSARY

annex - to take land and add it to a nation.

attorney general - the chief law officer of a national or state government.

cabinet - a group of advisers chosen by the president to lead government departments.

censure (SEHNT-shuhr) - to officially express disapproval.

civil war - a war between groups in the same country. The United States of America and the Confederate States of America fought a civil war from 1861 to 1865.

Constitution - the laws that govern the United States. Something relating to or following the laws of a constitution is constitutional.

debate - a contest in which two sides argue for or against something.

Democrat - a member of the Democratic political party. When John Tyler was president, Democrats supported farmers and landowners.

devolve - to be handed down or transferred.

eulogy (YOO-luh-jee) - a writing or a speech in honor of someone who has died.

inauguration (ih-naw-gyuh-RAY-shuhn) - a ceremony in which a person is sworn into office.

militia (muh-LIH-shuh) - a group of citizens trained for war or emergencies.

secede - to break away from a group.

secretary of state - a member of the president's cabinet who handles relations with other countries.

slogan - a word or a phrase used to express a position, a stand, or a goal.

unconstitutional - something that goes against the laws of a constitution.

War of 1812 - from 1812 to 1814. A war fought between the United States and Great Britain over shipping rights and the capture of U.S. soldiers.

Whig - a member of a political party that was very strong in the early 1800s but ended in the 1850s. Whigs supported laws that helped business.

WEB SITES

To learn more about John Tyler, visit ABDO Publishing Company on the World Wide Web at **www.abdopublishing.com**. Web sites about John Tyler are featured on our Book Links page. These links are routinely monitored and updated to provide the most current information available.

INDEX